From Adam to Easter

THE STORY OF EASTER FOR CHILDREN

WRITTEN BY ERIC BOHNET

ILLUSTRATED BY MICHELLE DORENKAMP

When God created all the world,

He saw that it was good.

No one sinned and no one died;

All did just as they should.

And best of all, God made a man,

In His own image formed.

God's breath of life had filled his lungs,

And Adam was transformed.

But this perfection did not last;
It broke when Adam sinned.
He ate the fruit to be like God,
While that old serpent grinned.

From this rebellion, all mankind
Would live under a curse.
They'd all be born with sinful hearts,
And things would soon get worse.

With sin came death and toil and sweat,
And untold misery.
All because of one man's sin
And eating from that tree.

But God still loved His children, so
He promised that someday
He'd send a second Adam, who
Would take our sins away.

This promise was repeated long,
Through prophets whom God sent.
They told of One who was to come
For all our benefit.

No man could pay the price for sin;
The cost was far too steep.
Our only hope was in the Lord
And in His love so deep.

So God sent Jesus, His own Son,
Who was His Word made flesh,
To be a man, fulfill the Law,
To die and conquer death.

He came to Earth to live with men
And teach them of God's love.
He told how God would forgive sin
And give us heaven above.

The devil came again to tempt

This second perfect man.

But Jesus wouldn't fall for lies.

With God, He made His stand.

He knew He had to suffer long

For those who had rebelled.

He hung for hours on the cross

To save us all from hell.

At last, He knew the price was paid.

His suffering was done.

"It's finished," He did loudly cry;

Then died, for He had won.

With Jesus' death came grace and life;
From death we all were freed.
For Jesus paid the price for sin
By dying on that tree.

On Easter, Jesus rose again
To lead us through the strife.
As Adam's sin had brought us death,
So Jesus brought us life.

And since that day, though men still sin,
Through Christ we are forgiven.
So when we die, we'll live again
Fore'er with Him in heaven.

Dear Parents,

The apostle Paul's letters to the Romans and the Corinthians teach about the concept of the First Adam, who disobeyed God, and the Second (sometimes called the Last) Adam, who obeyed Him.

This Arch Book helps to explain a connection between the Old Testament and the New: that the first man's first sin brought havoc and despair to mankind, and then Jesus' life, death, and resurrection completed the act of reconciling us to God. The First Adam's sin brought death; Jesus' death brought eternal life. Paul eloquently explains the parallels and symmetry of this fulfillment: "But the free gift is not like the trespass. For if many died through one man's trespass, much more have the grace of God and the free gift by the grace of that one man Jesus Christ abounded for many. And the free gift is not like the result of that one man's sin. For the judgment following one trespass brought condemnation, but the free gift following many trespasses brought justification. For if, because of one man's trespass, death reigned through that one man, much more will those who receive the abundance of grace and the free gift of righteousness reign in life through the one man Jesus Christ" (Romans 5:15–17).

After you read this book with your child, look also at a children's Bible and explain how all the books in it serve to tell the big story of God's people, of God's love, and of God's promise of forgiveness, mercy, and salvation through faith in Christ Jesus. Explain that Christ's love and mercy are far greater than Adam's original sin, and that although we inherited that original sin, we are the beloved children of God, adopted through Christ, and that means we inherited His kingdom as well.

The Editor